Rhymes and Tales

Bernard J. Weiss
Senior Author
Reading and Linguistics

Susan B. Cruikshank
Reading and Language Arts

Eldonna L. Evertts
Language Arts

Loreli Olson Steuer
Reading and Linguistics

Lyman C. Hunt
General Editor—Satellite Books

Holt
Basic
Reading

Level 3

HOLT, RINEHART AND WINSTON, PUBLISHERS
New York • Toronto • Mexico City • London • Sydney • Tokyo

ISBN 0-03-061383-3
789 071 98765

Art Credits:

Marika, pages 4 – 17, 38 – 49
Karen Ackoff, pages 18 – 25
Sally Springer, pages 26 – 33
Maggie Zander, pages 34 – 37
Joseph Veno, pages 50 – 53
Pam Ford, pages 54 – 63
Cover art by James Endicott

Table of Contents

Books 5

A Book Helps 10

The Big Book 14

The Bears 18

The Bears Cook 22

B Was a Book   *a poem by Edward Lear* 25

The Pigs 26

The Pigs Play 30

LANGUAGE: Making New Words 33

One, Two, Three   *a poem* 34

A Play 38

The Three Little Pigs 42

LANGUAGE: Books, Bears, and Pigs 50

Don Reads 54

NEW WORDS 64

Books

Linda has books.

Jim has books.

Linda has big books.

Big books are fun.

Jim has little books.

Little books are fun.

Books are big.

Books are little.

Books are fun.

A Book Helps

Pedro has a big book.

Pedro reads a big book.

A big book helps Pedro.

Pat has a little book.

Pat reads a little book.

A little book helps Pat.

Pedro reads a big book.

Pat reads a little book.

A big book helps Pedro.

A little book helps Pat.

The Big Book

Pat has a big book.

Pat reads the big book.

Jim reads the big book.

Pat reads to Jim.

Jim cooks.

The big book helps Jim.

Jim has fun.

Jim reads to Pat.

Pat cooks.

The big book helps Pat.

Pat has fun.

Pat reads to Jim.

Jim reads to Pat.

Pat and Jim cook.

The book helps Pat and Jim.

The Bears

Don has a big book.

Bears are in the book.

The little bear has fun.

Don sees one little bear.
Don sees two big bears.

One, two, three!
Three bears are in the book.

Don reads the book.
Don reads to Pat and Jim.

Pat reads the book.

Pat sees the bears in the book.

Jim reads the book.

Jim sees the bears in the book.

One, two, three!

Three bears are in the book.

Don reads.

Pat reads to Don and Jim.

Jim reads.

Books are fun!

The little bear sees the big bears.

The Bears Cook

Two bears are in a house.

The two big bears cook.

The big bears cook in the house.

"Come in, little bear.
Come in the house.
Come and cook."

The little bear helps the big bears.

The little bear cooks.

The three bears cook.

The little bear has fun.

B Was a Book

B was a book
With a binding of blue,
And pictures and stories
For me and for you.
　Nice little book!

　　　　—Edward Lear

The Pigs

Meg has a book.

Meg looks in the book.

Meg sees pigs in the book.

One, two, three!

Meg sees three pigs in the book.

The three pigs are little.

Pat and Jim come in.

Pat looks in the book.

Jim looks in the book.

One, two, three!

Pat and Jim see the three pigs.

The pigs are little.

Meg reads and likes the book.

Pat likes the book.

Jim likes the three pigs.

The Pigs Play

Two little pigs are in a house.

One little pig plays.

"Come, two little pigs.

Come and play."

One little pig is in the house.
Two little pigs play.

"Come, little pig.
Come and play."

One little pig plays.

Two little pigs play.

Three little pigs play.

Making New Words

book
cook
look
hook

pig
big
wig
dig

Pat has a wig.

Jim took a book.

Meg and Don dig.

Initial Consonant Substitution. Have the pictures identified and each column of words read, calling attention to the initial consonant substitution. Then direct the children to match the sentences with the correct pictures.

33

One, Two, Three

One book,

Two books,

One, two, three!

Big books,

Little books,

Little books to see.

One book,
Two books,
One, two, three!

Little books,

Big books,

Big books to see.

A Play

Jim and Pat are in a play.

Meg and Don are in a play.

The play is <u>The Three Little Pigs.</u>

A wolf is in the play.

Jim plays the wolf.

Three little pigs are in the play.

Pat plays one little pig.

Meg and Don play two little pigs.

Bob helps Jim and Pat.

Bob helps Meg and Don.

The Three Little Pigs

One pig has a little house.

The pig is in the little house.

A wolf sees the little house.

The wolf looks for the pig.

The wolf looks in the little house.

The wolf sees the pig.

The pig sees the wolf.

Good-by, little house.

One pig has a big house.

The pig is in the big house.

The wolf sees the big house.

The wolf looks for the pig.

The wolf looks in the big house.

The wolf sees the pig.

The pig sees the wolf.

Good-by, big house.

One pig has a big, big house.

The pig is in the big, big house.

The wolf sees the big, big house.

The wolf looks for the pig.

The wolf looks in the big, big house.

The wolf sees the pig.

The pig sees the wolf.

Good-by, wolf!

Books, Bears, and Pigs

Sentence Meaning and Following Directions. In this selection, children show their understanding of the meaning of sentences by following directions. On pages 52 and 53, direct the children to read the sentences and do what they say.

Books are big.

Books are little.

Pigs are in books.

Bears are in books.

Look for one little book.

  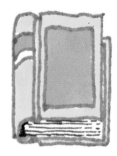

Look for two big bears.

Look for three little pigs.

Look for three big books.

Look for one little bear.

Look for two big pigs.

Don Reads

Don reads a book.

Goldilocks is in the book.

Goldilocks and the Three Bears

Goldilocks sees a little house.

Goldilocks looks in the house.

Goldilocks likes the little house.

Goldilocks is in the house.

Goldilocks sees three 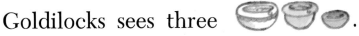.

Two are big.

One is little.

Goldilocks likes the little one.

Goldilocks sees three 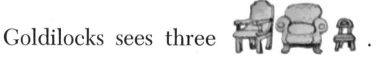 .

Two are big.

One is little.

Goldilocks likes the little one.

Goldilocks sees three beds.

Two are big.

One is little.

Goldilocks likes the little one.

The three bears come to the little house.

The bears see the three  .

The bears see the little ⬭ .

The little bear looks in the ⬭ .

The bears see the three .

The bears see the little .

The bears see the three beds.

The bears see the little bed.

The bears see Goldilocks!

Goldilocks is in the bed.

The bears see Goldilocks in the bed.

"Good-by, three bears."

"Good-by, Goldilocks."

New Words

The words listed beside the page numbers below appear in *Rhymes and Tales*, Level 3 in the HOLT BASIC READING SERIES. The words marked with an asterisk were introduced in *Hear, Say, See, Write!*, Level 2. The words printed in italics are easily decoded.

5. books* *cooks** 28. *see*

6. Linda* 17. *cook** 29. likes

 has*   and* 30. play

 *Jim** 18. bears *pig*

7. *big**   *Don*   *plays*

 are*   *in*   31. is

 *fun** 19. sees 39. wolf

8. little*   one* 41. *Bob*

10. a*   two* 43. for

 *book** *bear* 44. good-by

 helps* three* 52. *look*

11. Pedro* 22. house 55. Goldilocks

 reads* 23. come 59. *beds*

12. *Pat** 26. *pigs* 62. *bed*

14. the*   *looks*

15. to*   *Meg*